A
COMMEMORATIVE DISCOURSE
PREACHED AT THE FUNERAL
OF
THOMAS W. LOCKWOOD,
THURSDAY, APRIL 26th, 1866,
IN THE
WESTMINSTER CHURCH, DETROIT,
BY THE
Rev. G. WENDELL PRIME.

DETROIT, MICH.:
THE DAILY POST BOOK AND JOB PRINTING COMPANY,
(CORNER OF SHELBY AND LARNED STREETS.)
1866.

A MEMORIAL

OF

Thomas Wallace Lockwood,

OF DETROIT,

WHO DIED APRIL 24th, 1866.

DISCOURSE.

1 John ii, 17:—And the world passeth away, and the lust thereof; but he that doeth the will of God abideth forever.

When Job's three friends heard of all this evil that was come upon him, they came every one from his own place to mourn with him and to comfort him. They sat down with him upon the ground seven days and seven nights, and none spake a word unto him; for they saw that his grief was very great. Those who have gathered in the shadow of a mighty sorrow know the weight of that silence which reveals what is unutterable, the power of that stillness which is our only answer to the voice of God. "I was dumb, I opened not my mouth because thou didst it."

Such voiceless hours of waiting with the fatherless, upon the Almighty Father, have been passed with the grateful consciousness of your prayerful sympathy. And now it is fit that this silence should be broken.

It is in the observance of no formal custom that I would turn your attention unto thoughts divine, that seem to glow in the darkness of this mysterious bereavement. If you loved and respected him, whose memory has drawn you hither, you will receive, with tender consideration, that impression of God's truth, which was wrought into the very texture of his faithful heart.

Every stroke of death that cuts down some one at our side, lays open our hearts to the truth that "the world passeth away, and the lust thereof." But far more than this is written upon the door that closes on such a life as ended with the last moments of our beloved friend. From within the veil, we hear the glorious antithesis, the only strength of the living heart. These departing footfalls, on the pathway that leads outward and onward into the unseen and eternal, echo in our souls,—not only the frailty of earth, but with equal clearness,—the glory of the incorruptible and unfading. They tell us, not only that "the world passeth away, and the lust thereof," but also, that "he that doeth the will of God, abideth forever." You who have known this consistent servant of God, and follower of the Redeemer, if you have known him well, cannot fail to see this blessed truth so clearly, that it seems written in the heavens that have opened their doors for his ascended spirit.

"He that doeth the will of God, abideth forever."

When the world passeth away so evidently, the foundations seem to be broken up. When our hearts are wrung with anguish, love itself seems ruinous. When every hope and purpose is changed or frustrated, it seems as though it were folly to have any vital interests or earnest labor. Beauty is a cloud, and the sun is already setting. Life is a thought, and memory is already failing. What is there here, that we should rise and press onward, lay hold and struggle. Does it not all perish with the using? Shall we not weep the more, the more we see? Shall we not ache the more, the more we love? Shall we not sink the deeper, the farther we venture upon waves that cover as well as bear? Yes, the world passeth away, and the lust thereof; but that is not all—that is not the beginning. See, and believe, in the presence of this form, that leaves you not without reminding you of what its spirit held, "he that doeth the will of God, abideth forever." Nothing to that man, is in vain. However short or long his course, it is invariably complete and glorious. Seeking *first* the kingdom of God and his righteousness, all other things are added unto him; and however other things pass away, his kingdom is not of this world, and with his King, therefore, he reigns forever.

The soul of that man, who humbly gives himself up to the will of the Almighty, is like the cloudless firmament that has bent above us during every hour since this spirit fled. Looking upward, we behold bright towers of pillared clouds, glowing fountains of rosy flames, black tempests borne onward with the unseen fury of mighty winds; all these changing and interchanging with the light and darkness, calm and storm. And yet through all, there is no change in the measureless dome of silent distance that encloses all. This deep sea of heaven is always there in its infinite repose, and when the mists and veilings are swept away, we stand beneath the same calm smile and symbol of God's protection. We know that is there through all that blasts and falls. The clouds and darkness vanish, but the firmament abides forever. Before, around, within the soul, there is much that gathers, darkens, brightens, changes; but when all these pains and pleasures are swept away into the abyss, the spirit shines with a glory that is fadeless. "The world passeth away, and the lust thereof; but he that doeth the will of God, abideth forever."

In his life, in his walk, in his spirit, in the general impression and unconscious influence of his person and character, we have always felt that this truth was strongly set forth by him, for whom this world has now passed away.

Thomas Wallace Lockwood was born on the 11th of November, 1817. His early life was spent in Albany, where he was admitted to the Bar a few days before he was twenty-one years of age. Very soon after, he removed to this city, and here continued in the active duties of his profession until a few weeks before his death.

Many of you are familiar with every month of his growing influence, and know well the estimation in which he was held, with a unanimity certainly most rare, in this world of groundless hostilities and selfish disregard. You know the positions of trust that he has occupied, and you know, also, that for such a man as he to occupy them, was to be certain that in so doing he simply acquiesced in the desire of others. Although retiring in disposition, and disposed to undervalue his own endeavors, he never shrank from any labor that was for the advantage of his friends, the city, and the State. Those who know the nature of what gives form and facility to the administration of justice, who appreciate the benefit of what tends to elevate the character of the community, will always remember the faithful and efficient labors of our departed friend. This is the time to speak of what he was, rather than of what he did.

He was, through youth and manhood, one of the purest and most guileless of men. He was so *true*, that all believed in him instinctively, and yet he was so *kind*, that, as far as I can ascertain, every one who knew him remembers him with the most affectionate respect. We make this record of a man who was actively engaged in all the personal and public interests that bring others into the heat of conflict. There are few, indeed, so gifted by nature and grace as to guide their vessel through this length of voyage, and then sail into the harbor with such snowy sails. In speaking of those qualities that are manifest in the general intercourse of life, I will not say that he was liberal, for that word, in its popular sense, would be a detraction when applied to this quality in him. To my certain knowledge, in regard to all that a man can do for the benefit of others, he was not liberal, but actually—sacrificial. He did and he gave, not merely freely, but so that he felt it, so that it required some real self-denial in order to meet the desires of his heart for others. You cannot expect me to speak of those phases of his life and character that are revealed in the closest relations and holiest ties. Were it not for you, my beloved people, I should have refrained from attempting this tribute and its lessons, on the ground of my being his brother by adoption, and too near him in affection, to think of lifting up my voice above him in this hour of parting. But I am your servant, for Jesus' sake, and you know how cheerfully I would expend my own last breath for your profit or your comfort, in this vale of tears.

He was a father, affectionate as wise; a son that was never an anxiety, and always a solace and a joy; a husband that nourished and cherished as the Lord his church.

And yet all this would not be enough to bring peace to our souls in this hour of trial, could we not say, with a glorying that is in naught but the cross of Jesus—Behold! he liveth not unto himself, but unto Him who died for him and rose again. His trust is in no natural grace of character, nor any habit of rightful dealing. He is a follower of the only Redeemer; his righteousness is the obedience of the well-beloved Son; his grace is the humble dependence of a sinful man, who obeys the voice of the high calling of God in Christ Jesus. Whatever there was in him to inspire regard, to secure confidence, to bestow as a priceless heritage to his children, all this was not to the glory of himself, but, by his consistent profession of the Christian faith, to the glory of his Creator and Redeemer.

For seven years he was an Elder of this church, and blessed is that church who can have so pure, so strong and so acceptable a man as this, to assist in its spiritual administration. His presence in these councils will remain with me as long as it is mine to exercise this ministry of reconciliation. His work in this service was continued after illness had withdrawn him from secular pursuits. Upon his bed he listened to the confessions of faith, and welcomed to the communion of the church on earth. From the beginning, his hand and heart were warmly engaged in everything that pertained to the interests of this organization. You who bent with anxious toil in planting this little vine, know how much its existence, growth and fruitfulness are owing to his faithfulness and zeal. Humanly speaking, his loss to this church is irreparable. His name can never be forgotten here. No tablet need mark what is written on living hearts, so long as we and ours sit together in these heavenly places in Christ Jesus.

And it would not be justice to his memory were I to omit the statement, that there was no peculiarity nor defect in his life and character that was at all at variance with the possession of these precious gifts. This is only the beginning of what might be told of his quiet, persevering energy, his unselfish, patient, thoughtful, happy, loving spirit. Doubtless, you would like to know something of those hours when the flame flickered, and what we saw when it gleamed again for precious moments, on our searching eyes and aching hearts. But all this is utterly impossible to-day and here. How can I at this moment, and in this presence, speak of that voice which gave me a welcome on that fair morning when I first trod these city streets; that hand which led me five short years ago to a second home, now hallowed by a precious memory and most sacred sorrow. For all this I have now no strength, but in the mighty power of that truth which he believed and loved, there is a purpose which enables me to stand beside him even here, and speak of what was magnified both by his life and by his death. As long as it is mine to preach these unsearchable riches of Christ, may God keep me from any love and any sorrow that would so unnerve my heart and tongue that I could not lift up before your desiring eyes this Cross and our Redeemer. Though nothing seems more keenly distressful to hearts of love than temporary separation by the dark flood of death, still there is nothing on earth so exalting and so exultant as the perfect confidence of the living in the eternal triumph of a ransomed soul.

My frame has thrilled, when seeing in the memorable past, that great procession, which, twice in a decade, wound along the shore of the Ægean, drew near the gates of Athens, and soon ascended the grooved pavement at the summit of the Acropolis.

Passing through massive doors of bronze, swung between columns of Pentelic marble, it moves through the corridor of glowing pillars, shining in the sunlight like the gates of Day. Borne aloft at the front of all this moving splendor, in the centre of that architectural magnificence which an admiring world has never equalled, waved the banner of banners, the sacred robe of the country's Goddess, the Crocus-colored Peplon. Its brilliant tissue shone with rich embroideries of fabled conflicts, and the mighty ones of history and of song. Among these illustrious pictures were those heroes that had won signal victories for their native land. It was the acme of human exaltation to perform such achievements as to win a place among these noble forms, and be thus borne in triumph to the centre of the citadel, and left upon the statue of gold and ivory that looked down from that sacred height upon the capital of Greece. *That* was the only glory worthy of the name in the highest civilization of which the heathen world can boast. My brethren, you who believe in the promise of life in Christ Jesus, who know that the life that is hid with him in God shall appear with him in glory, what is all that was embalmed in the friezes of the Parthenon, by the genius of Phidias, when it is seen in the light of this divine assurance: "The world passeth away and the lust thereof; but he that doeth the will of God, abideth forever."

What is that will? Is it an abstraction? Is it a mere opinion of those who assume to be the interpreters of the mind of God? Is it whatever the heart of man suggests to itself, as its own preference for time and for eternity?

This solemn question we cannot decide for others, but you, my friends, who loved this Christian man, and united with him in the interests of this church, you have acknowledged, in some degree, what you consider God's Holy Will. You know the source from which we have these words "he that doeth the will of God, abideth forever." From that same source, you know well, that His will is made known in its fullness only in the person and work of His image and His Son.

This assurance of abiding forever has all its strength in Him who lost his life for such words as these, "No man cometh unto the Father but by *me*—*I* am the bread of life—Whosoever liveth and believeth in *me*, shall never die." Whatever may be the confidence, the delusions, the fate of others, you, my brethren, have learned too much of God's Word, and felt too much of His spirit, to be able to find *your* peace in any will that is not the will of God in Christ. You cannot know an hour of satisfaction until you have fulfilled all His blessed will. This is the penalty of your enlightenment; this is the working of His truth; this is the gracious compulsion by which He leads you to Himself.

Will any one of you hesitate longer as to the degree in which this will of God shall be done by you? It is not a requirement that exacts a rigid acquiescence in ceremonial forms. It is not a conventional school of morality, with whose arbitrary tenets you are desired to comply. Was there anything like this in the man whom we now mourn, as he illustrates in death the brightness of this life of faith and its blessed ending? No! The will of God that we are to do, brings us all alike in the way of humble penitence, faith, acknowledgment and true endeavor. Love, love only, is the fulfilling of the law. Love of God, one another in Him, and all in Christ.

He that does *His will* abides forever! Forever in the hearts of those who remember his godly walk, his genial smile, his manly tenderness, and his prayerful spirit; forever in the souls of his children, his friends, and all, who through them receive the benefit of a Christ-like following through this network of worldliness and evil; forever in the eternal increase of that glory which fills his spirit, who is risen with his Saviour from the dead. What an immeasurable blessedness to know and feel this through all the wear and weakness of trial, affliction, disease, gradual decay, or sudden dissolution. Ought not the thought to nerve our hearts for whatever is agonizing and inevitable in the march of death?

Do I speak to one who cares for none of these things, whose heart is so contented or engaged that he feels no desire for any renewal of its nature or its strength? The time is not distant when you shall feel the river of death rolling beneath your feet, and the heat of pain breaking up the icy crust on which you stand a few brief moments before you sink away forever in the chilling flood. Would this assurance have no value then, when every nerve and faculty of your sentient being strives, with consuming fire, to brand upon your soul its helplessness and agony? In the presence of all this weakness and woe, do you not see why we need something more than mere principles and philosophy to build up the spirit, warm its affections, and stay it upon its God? What is there, in all that is offered you by the world and the wisdom of man, to bring you into His fellowship who, of God, is made unto us, Wisdom and Righteousness, and Sanctification, and Redemption? When all the life-springs of your own nature are dried away, as the hand of Time cuts down the trees and foliage that now shade the channels of your being, believe, not a child in this faith, but its Author and Finisher, believe that there is, then and now, no living water for a thirsting spirit, save at the fountain that is opened in this Rock of Ages—whosover will, let him take the water of life freely.

Take it most freely ye who have been most sorely smitten by this painful blow. It came upon you at the fountain. You need not ascend into heaven, to bring Christ down from above, nor descend into the deep, to bring up Christ from the dead. The word is nigh thee, even in thy mouth and in thy heart. It speaks in this hour of anguish: Fear not, I am with thee. Lean, this side, once wounded, is now strong and near thee. Sink, if thou desirest, this arm surrounds thee. Rest, now and forever, for in me thou shalt have peace.

Proceedings of the Detroit Bar.

A meeting of the Detroit Bar was held on the afternoon of the 24th instant, in the Bar Library, to take appropriate action on the death of Hon. THOMAS W. LOCKWOOD. The attendance was large. The meeting was called to order by A. D. Fraser, Esq.

Hon. George E. Hand opened with a few fitting remarks. All knew, he said, for what purpose those present had assembled. An honored member of the Bar had taken his departure from earth. It had been his lot to be acquainted with Mr. LOCKWOOD from his first arrival in the city, and he had known him only to esteem him and admire his excellent and attractive traits of character. He was a high-minded, honorable and candid practitioner, and enjoyed the respect and confidence of all with whom he came in contact. As a lawyer, Mr. LOCKWOOD was well read and well balanced, and his irreproachable integrity was shown in all his professional life. In all relations in life he always sustained himself with propriety and honor. The deceased was an only son, and being judiciously reared, reached manhood, having undergone fewer trials and misfortunes than are usually passed through by young men. Coming here just on the verge of manhood, Mr. LOCKWOOD, by his uniform courtesy and candor, rapidly won the good opinion of all. At the time of his decease, he was in the prime of life, at a period of unusual professional activity. His record is an honorable one, and he has passed away with as few enemies and as many friends as any member of the Bar in the city, and his memory will ever remain fresh in the hearts of his associates.

D. Bethune Duffield, Esq., continued as follows:

Mr. CHAIRMAN,

I can not tell just how sadly this announcement may affect other members of the Bar, but I know that it puts into my heart a peculiar sorrow. For more than twenty-five years past, in political, professional and social life, I have walked side by side, and almost hand in hand, with our departed brother, and may, therefore, appropriately bear testimony to his worth. All who have labored in this forum thus long, will, I doubt not, frankly say with me, that however professionally opposed they may have been with him whom we now mourn, they never experienced the least approach to anything like a personal strife, or even a harsh difference. Firm, and properly tenacious of his clients' rights, as he always was, he was, nevertheless, just and fair in the maintenance of them—never misleading by misrepresentation, never over-reaching even when holding the post of advantage. His professional intercourse was always genial, and if not manifested in warm demonstrations or large professions, we all well knew that his was a reliable and worthy friendship, and that his professional record was as clean as that of the high-minded Christian gentleman, who conscientiously puts honor above interest, right above gain, and truth above everything. In saying this of our departed friend, I am aware I bear to him high testimony, and the full value of it you will appreciate; for your own experience tells you that this profession, in which we all labor, is surrounded by more and stronger temptations than almost any other, and of which the outside world knows very little; yet you will all admit that our friend Lockwood seemed to have adopted and to have had fulfilled to him the precept so appropriate to us all, "Keep innocency, and take heed unto the thing that is right, for *that* shall bring you peace at the last."

In political life, Mr. Lockwood was earnest, laborious and unselfish. Few men of his years have labored more faithfully under a party banner than did he under his—from the ward caucus down to and through the grand quadrennial battles. Yet he never appeared clamorous by claiming the rewards of office; nay, more, when the claims of his Country called with a louder voice than that of party, he marched boldly forth from under his party flag, and, placing himself beneath the broad flag of the Union, resolved that he would know no party until that precious ensign of our liberties had triumphed over all its enemies. A man of earnest convictions, he had the strength and courage to carry them out, let them lead whithersoever they would; *provided,* always, it was not from the path of Patriotism and Truth.

While serving in our State Legislature, he was untiring in his duties, and on the Judiciary Committee of the House, did much for us all, in the investigations appropriate to this laborious place. His name will be long remembered throughout the State by the members of the last three Legislatures, by his friends of the Bar at large, as well as by all those who sympathized with his political opinions and principles.

As a Citizen, no man was more faithful to the public interests than he. Did public disturbance of any kind occur, he was always among the first to appear and range himself on the side of good order, and in the support of Government. Nor in any measure of public improvement or reform was he ever found lacking, either in personal effort or contribution. In every sense of the word, and to its fullest meaning, he was *a valuable citizen,* one whom we could ill afford to spare, and whose vacant place will, I fear, long remain unfilled. The City of Detroit owes a large debt of gratitude to the quiet but efficient efforts in her behalf, through the twenty years just past in the life of the Hon. THOMAS W. LOCKWOOD.

As one of the earliest and most active members of the Young Men's Benevolent Society, too, he will long be remembered, and his name blessed by the aged poor who yet linger among us. As a friend in social life, we all know how courteous, hospitable and amiable he was in all his intercourse, and how wide a gap his departure makes in the extended circle of his many friends.

But he has gone, and we shall no more greet that face, so handsome in youth, so pleasant and cheerful even to the last. As I sat by his bedside a few nights since, watching and aiding him in his struggle with the terrible fever which seemed to be burning the very life from his enfeebled body, he appeared the same courteous, well-mannered gentleman that he always was. Feeble and faint though he was, he was not too feeble to render audible and polite acknowledgment for the most trifling efforts on his behalf, thus showing how the traits of the true gentleman lingered and shone in him to the very last.

We say farewell to him at a time when Death seems to be again girding himself for busy activity on the earth. He is busy abroad, busy at home, busy here among us, and as my thoughts run back over the last quarter of a century, during which our friend has here walked in our company, oh! how busy does he seem to have been in bearing away the members of this Bar! How many graves rise this day into view, filled by those who were once our friends and fellow-laborers here! and still we are opening new sepulchres; still rearing fresh monuments! One by one, like the white sea-birds by the shore, our companions rise and disappear over the great ocean of life, and we see them no more. Soon we too must take wing. Let us see to it, my brethren and friends, that when life shall close with us, our record may be found as pure and unspotted as was that of THOMAS W. LOCKWOOD.

I move, Mr. Chairman, that a committee of five be appointed to frame and report to this meeting resolutions expressive of the feelings of the Bar on this occasion.

The following gentlemen were requested, by the Chairman, to act as such committee: D. B. Duffield, W. Jennison, Jr., C. I. Walker, Levi Bishop, and D. C. Holbrook.

After a short conference, they reported the following:

WHEREAS, The death of the Hon. THOMAS W. LOCKWOOD, a member of this Bar, has recently transpired, while he was yet in the prime of life, in the midst of usefulness, and actively engaged in the duties of his profession, it is therefore by the Bar of Detroit

RESOLVED, That his death awakens in us all emotions of profound sorrow and regret, not only because of the rupture of professional ties, now consecrated by the friendship of many years, but also for the reason that his early removal from active life is attended with the laceration of many hearts, both within his own home circle and the wide field of his numerous friends throughout the city and State.

RESOLVED, That we record in all sincerity our conviction that this, our friend and brother, whose long connection with this Bar had given us ample opportunity to test his worth, was, in every sense of the word, a sound, upright and honorable lawyer, a truly valuable fellow citizen, prompt in the support of every reform at home, and every enterprise for the benefit of the State at large, a cordial and reliable friend, a devoted son, husband and father, and as a Christian, one whom all men testify kept himself "unspotted from the world."

Resolved, That we will long and affectionately remember the name and character of our departed brother, and, again associating it in hallowed memory with that of his early and lamented partner,* the fragrance of whose life still lingers in our professional walks, we will henceforth hold them both as synonymous with professional faithfulness, manly honor, and Christian integrity.

Resolved, That our hearty sympathy in this affliction is hereby extended to our much-respected fellow-citizen, the aged mother of the deceased, and to his sorrowing wife and children, who are called thus sadly to part with a truly-devoted son, husband and father; and that copies of these resolutions, duly attested, be transmitted to the mother and family of the deceased.

Resolved, That, as a tribute of our respect for the

* The late Samuel Barstow.

virtues and memory of the deceased, we will attend the funeral in a body.

The resolutions were unanimously adopted.

J. S. Newberry, Esq., offered the following, which was adopted:

RESOLVED, That the members of this Bar meet on Thursday, at the Library Rooms, at two o'clock, P. M., and thence proceed in a body to the late residence of the deceased to attend the funeral.

On Thursday morning, the 26th inst., before the closing of the morning session of the *Circuit Court*, William Jennison, Jr., Esq., moved the Court that the resolutions of the Bar, of day before yesterday, relative to the death of Hon. THOMAS W. LOCKWOOD, be spread upon the records of the Court, making some very appropriate remarks in support of his motion. The Court granted the motion, and his Honor Judge Witherell paid a tribute of respect and esteem to the memory of the deceased, and ordered the adjournment of the Court until the next day at half-past nine, A. M., as a token of respect to the deceased.

[At the funeral services of Mr. LOCKWOOD, there was in attendance from the members of the Bar and Judiciary, a larger delegation than had been witnessed for many years on similar occasions.]

Action of the Board of Trade.

At a meeting of the Board of Trade on the 26th inst., the following preamble and resolutions, relative to the death of Hon. Thomas W. Lockwood, were presented by J. G. Erwin, Esq., and unanimously adopted:—

Whereas, It has pleased an All-Wise Providence to remove by death the Hon. Thomas W. Lockwood, an honorary member of this association, and one to whom it has been largely indebted for acts of kindness and courtesy in his official capacity as a legislator of the people; be it therefore

Resolved, That in the death of Mr. Lockwood we deplore the loss of one whose unpretending life has illustrated the noblest virtues; the consistent Christian; the enlightened and liberal-minded public servant; the useful and exemplary citizen; the honest man; one who lived beloved, and died without reproach.

Resolved, That the Secretary is hereby instructed to transmit a copy of these resolutions to the family of the deceased.

Resolved, That as a further mark of respect, the association is hereby adjourned.

Action of the Presbytery of Michigan.

The Presbytery of Michigan met in Bennington, Shiawassee county, on Tuesday, April 24th, at seven P. M., and was opened with a sermon by Rev. R. S. Goodman, of Grand Rapids, at the request of the last Moderator, Rev. R. Kay. Rev. J. W. McGregor was chosen Moderator, and Rev. Richard Kay, Temporary Clerk.

A gloom pervaded its opening, at the announcement of the death, that morning, of Hon. T. W. Lockwood, of Detroit, and it was subsequently

Resolved, That the Presbytery are deeply afflicted in hearing of the death of Hon. T. W. Lockwood, an Elder in the Westminster Church, Detroit, whom we have esteemed as a gentleman of great personal worth, a consistent Christian, deeply interested in the cause of Christ, and ever ready to make sacrifices for its promotion; one to whom we owe much for the organization of our Church in Detroit, and for its support and defense in its time of need, and for his wisdom and faithfulness in the discharge of the duties of a Ruling Elder. We deeply sympathize with the Church, and with his afflicted family, in their great loss, and would direct them for consolation, where only we can find our own, that is, *in the assurance* that the Lord Jesus, the Great Head of the Church, is on the throne, and rules in righteousness and in goodness, for the sanctification and salvation of his people and his church, even where darkness surrounds him, and his dispensations remove the lights of our households, and those who rule in the Church and minister at her altars.

Westminster Church.

At a meeting of the congregation of this Church, on Friday evening, May 18th, 1866, the following minute was adopted:

A bereaved people, realizing their loss more keenly, from day to day, desire to express their deepening sense of deprivation in the eternal gain of their honored friend and brother, T. W. Lockwood, Esq., Ruling Elder of this Church.

We remember, with grateful affection, his wisdom, zeal and liberality in the organization of this communion, and his devoted adherence to its interests, to the last moments of his life.

It is the will of God in Christ Jesus concerning us, that in everything we should give thanks, and we now return to our Heavenly Father thanksgiving for having provided for us, in our times of need, this able, faithful servant, and for having spared him to see so much of the fruit of his labors.

Our hearts are so moved by this affliction, that we can truly endeavor to share the burden of this sorrow with the family of our beloved friend; and we desire to bow with them in the secret of His tabernacle, and patiently wait the salvation of the Lord.

By terrible things in righteousness hast thou answered us, O! God of our salvation, and may we hear thy voice calling us to higher devotion and greater zeal.

www.ingramcontent.com/pod-product-compliance
Lightning Source LLC
LaVergne TN
LVHW011123110826
845150LV00008B/2239
9781418195120